JOHN
God Became Flesh

ELIZABETH VIERA TALBOT

Pacific Press® Publishing Association
Nampa, Idaho
Oshawa, Ontario, Canada
www.pacificpress.com

Cover design by Gerald Lee Monks
Cover design resources from John Steel
Inside design by Aaron Troia
Outside editor: Aivars Ozolins
Jesus 101 logo designer: Steve Trapero

Copyright © 2010 by Pacific Press® Publishing Association
Printed in the United States of America

The author assumes full responsibility for the accuracy of all facts and quotations as cited in this book.

Unless otherwise noted, all Scripture quotations are from *The New American Standard Bible*®, copyright © 1960, 1962, 1963, 1968, 1971, 1972, 1973, 1975, 1977, 1995 by The Lockman Foundation. Used by permission.

Additional copies of this book are available by calling toll-free 1-800-765-6955 or by visiting http://www.AdventistBookCenter.com.

Library of Congress Cataloging-in-Publication Data:

Talbot, Elizabeth Viera.
  John : God became flesh / Elizabeth Viera Talbot.
     p. cm. — (Jesus101)
  ISBN 13: 978-0-8163-2403-3 (pbk.)
  ISBN 10: 0-8163-2403-4 (pbk.)
  1. Bible. N.T. John—Criticism, interpretation, etc. I. Title.
  BS2615.52.T35 2010
  226.5'06—dc22
                                          2010006201

13 14 • 5 4 3

Dedication

I dedicate this booklet to
my academic, ministerial, and spiritual mentors:

Dr. Lynn Losie
Dr. Andrew Lincoln
Dr. Mitch Henson
Dr. Smuts van Rooyen
Dr. Aivars Ozolins
Pastor Mark Papendick

To my husband, Patrick, whose passion
for the gospel continues to inspire me,
and to my parents who, since my
earliest childhood, instilled the
love of Jesus in me

And always to Jesus,
my Kinsman-Redeemer

Contents

The Beginning

A line of novelty products came on the market about twenty years ago: 3-D (three-dimensional) puzzles and pictures. Do you remember them? They came out in the form of books, posters, and other wall art. All I could see was a nice pattern of various colors, something like a paper tapestry. Other people insisted that they were seeing beautiful things, such as mountains, trees, eagles, and fish, in three dimensions. I wanted to see what they saw, but I didn't know how to focus my eyes to enter this other dimension. I wondered whether I needed special glasses.

Then my birthday came along, and the young adults of my church decided to give me one of those pictures as a gift. It was a large framed picture behind glass, ready to hang on the wall. Everyone in the group kept staring at the picture and commenting on the beauty of the scenery: pine trees, a full moon, an eagle's nest, and an adult eagle catching a salmon. As far as I could tell, everyone was making this up—but they were all describing the same scene, so I concluded that obviously I was the one with the problem.

Then someone took the time to teach me how to focus my eyes. They even taught me how to use the glass in front of the picture to learn to focus appropriately. When everyone had gone home, I decided to sit in front of the picture until I could see what they saw. I will never forget what happened next. As I followed the instructions I had been given, my eyes started to perceive a whole other reality within the picture that I had not previously seen. It was as if I had walked into the picture and could now see those things that the others claimed to see. I felt like part of the picture, looking around and seeing beautiful things; I was experiencing a more profound reality than the flat paper patterns that I had seen before. It was breathtaking!

The Gospel of John was written so that we may discover a whole new reality that exists beyond the one we normally perceive. In a way, this Gospel offers us a set of new glasses—the glasses of faith in Jesus—that are necessary for us to see what we normally can't see with our natural eyes. John proposes that there are two realities: the one we see literally with our physical eyes (often not very pleasant) and the divine reality we see through spiritual glasses. The bridge between the first and the second realities is faith in the person of Jesus, who He is, and what He accomplished. And, John says, when you see the second, more profound reality, you will behold the glory of God and the beauty and assurance of what Jesus has accomplished on your behalf: eternal life.

John introduces Jesus as much more than a prophet from God or a miracle worker. He wants us to see Jesus beyond His humanity. Throughout John's narrative, Jesus reveals Himself more fully through seven signs (not just miracles, but testimonies of who He is) and seven "I AM" statements: the Bread of Life (6:35); the Light of the world (8:12; 9:5); the Door (10:7); the Good Shepherd (10:11, 14); the Resurrection and the Life (11:25); the Way, the Truth, and the Life (14:6); and the True Vine (15:1).

Get ready for a breathtaking experience: God became flesh! And we are about to enter into the picture—so put on your 3-D glasses and BE AMAZED!

The Word was God!

Unlike Matthew and Luke, John does not narrate details of Jesus' birth. We don't even hear about Mary, Joseph, the angels, the shepherds, and the Magi. John's story starts long before the birth at "the beginning." He starts his Gospel with a deliberate reminder of the first words of the Bible in Genesis 1:1, which eventually became the name to the first book of the Bible. "In the beginning was the

Word, and the Word was with God, and the Word was God. He was in the beginning with God" (John 1:1, 2). Therefore, when we step into this 3-D picture, we step into an eternal picture of a pre-existing God. The Word was not created, but was God and was with God since the very beginning of the universe.

John introduces a God who was with God since the beginning but was distinct from God the Father. This is a bold statement with which to begin the Gospel because Judaism was, and is, a monotheistic religion. How could there be another God? Of course, Christianity is also a monotheistic religion that believes in one God manifested in Three Persons (Father, Son, and Holy Spirit). But this was a foreign concept for the Jewish community.

John's prologue (1:1–18) uses a literary device called *inclusio*. An *inclusio* is like a narrative sandwich: the text begins and ends in the same way. John's *inclusio* is that Jesus is God! And he mentions this very important fact both in verse 1 and in verse 18 of his introduction. As a matter of fact, the entire Gospel is an *inclusio* of Jesus' divinity, as the third and last assertion that Jesus is God is made after His resurrection (John 20:28).

Creation, life, and light

Now that John has deliberately used words that remind the reader of the creation of the world (John 1:1), he naturally continues with Creation language, and even with Creation order. "All things came into being through Him, and apart from Him nothing came into being that has come into being" (verse 3). The Word of God was the Agent through which everything was created. Genesis tells us that God spoke the world into existence (Genesis 1); He would say and it would be. The Word of God was the active Agent of creation. He Himself was Life (see John 1:4). He didn't just *give* life, but He *was* Life. And following the order of Creation, John talks about "light" (see Genesis 1:3–5); he says that the Word was life, and that life became "the Light of men" (John 1:4). And just as in Creation, when the Light appeared, darkness was exposed (verse 5). That Jesus is the Life and the Light are important premises that John repeats several times throughout the Gospel; they are also two of the seven "I AM" statements of Jesus (John 9:5; 11:25). The dualism of light and darkness, sight and blindness, is also a constant theme in this narrative because the entire Gospel is written to challenge the reader to believe in Jesus and, through the "glasses of faith," enter into a fuller understanding of reality. God is about to redeem His creation, and the story of redemption starts at "the beginning."

John goes on to say that Jesus "was the true Light which, . . . enlightens every man" (John 1:9). Every person has the chance to accept or reject the Light. Then we learn that when the Light came home, those at home did not receive Him. What a tragedy! Home is supposed to be your own place, where everybody knows your name. The Word, the Life-Giver, and Light Bearer "was in the world, and the world was made through Him, and the world did not know Him. He came to His own, and those who were His own did not receive Him" (verses 10, 11). This is the bad news. But there is also good news.

Some did accept the Light. And to those who received Him by believing in Him, He gave a gift: a new status—children of God. Those who believe in Him are *given* the right to become children of God! Have you ever been rejected by your own family, your own home? God invites you to join the heavenly family. No one can take you away from Him. When you receive the Light, darkness dissipates, and you become a child, not born of passion or the will of a man, but of the will of God. You have a home. And your Father knows your name.

The new tabernacle

Are you enjoying a 3-D picture yet? Well, keep those glasses of faith on because there is much more to come! The beauty of God's revelation in Jesus Christ is breathtaking!

Until now we don't really know who the Word is. We just know that the Word was with God in the beginning and that the Word was God. Now we are about to see one of the most amazing mysteries in the 3-D picture of the universe. "The Word became flesh, and dwelt among us, and we saw His glory, glory as of the only begotten from the Father, full of grace and truth" (verse 14). Wow! Unbelievable! The eternal God became flesh. The Word became human. This is the mystery that we call the *Incarnation:* God becoming one of us in order to redeem us. So, says John, when you see Jesus, notice the profound reality that the eternal God of Creation is in a human form. God has moved into our neighborhood.

The words used in this verse are of the utmost importance. First, John's choice of the word *flesh* is designed to highlight the fact that the Word did not make just a spiritual appearance but had a real physical body. Jesus is fully God and fully man. Second, the word *dwelt* means that He encamped or, in the Old Testament vernacular, *tabernacled* among us. This is a key word because it derives from the root word *tabernacle,* the sanctuary in the wilderness, the place where God's presence resided with His people. John wants his readers to catch the connection and to understand that the term refers back to the tabernacle that Moses built in the wilderness. Immediately, he uses another word, *glory,* which is also from the tabernacle vocabulary: "Then the cloud covered the tent of meeting, and the glory of the LORD filled the tabernacle" (Exodus 40:34). Now the tabernacle is the flesh, and we see God's glory through Jesus Christ. He is the fullest revelation of the glory of God. Furthermore, His utmost glory is the Cross, where God is revealed most fully. A basic outline of the Gospel of John highlights this fact:

Prologue	1:1–18
Book of signs	1:19–12:50
Book of glory	13:1–20:31
Epilogue	21:1–25

The central two books or sections in this Gospel highlight *who* Jesus is (through His signs and testimonies) and the realities that were manifested in *His glory* at the Cross. Jesus' passion is repeatedly described as His glorification (John 12:23; 13:31, 32; 17:1, 4).

Now, we no longer just *hear* the Word of God speaking new worlds into existence, but we *see* the Word of God because He walks among us. And what do we see? Oh, says John, wait until I tell you! We see *grace* and *truth*! We see more clearly than before! Grace is mentioned in three sentences in John's prologue. Moses had received a partial revelation of God's grace and truth (see Exodus 34:6). Now, through Jesus, we are *seeing* grace and truth fully realized. John uses the word *truth* twenty-five times in this Gospel; and Jesus will utter one of His seven "I AM" statements claiming to be the Truth: " 'I am the way, and the truth, and the life; no one comes to the Father but through Me' " (John 14:6). When we wear our "faith glasses," we can see clearly that the Truth is the Person of Jesus.

Can you see Him now?

The remainder of John's prologue is devoted to highlighting the supreme excellence of Jesus as a Revealer of God. Yes, God has revealed Himself in the past, but now He has surpassed that revelation because Jesus is the only One who can fully reveal the Father: "The Law was given through Moses; grace and truth were realized through Jesus Christ. No one has seen God at any time; the only begotten God who is in the bosom of the Father, He has explained Him" (John 1:17, 18).

Moses was a mediator of God's revelation. Jesus is not just the mediator but the embodiment of God. And now we are beginning to see the beautiful scenery in the 3-D picture: grace and truth in the fullest sense. Jesus is the utmost Revealer of God. The *theophanies* or revelations of God in the Old Testament were shadows of the Son who fully reveals the Father. One of John's major recurring themes is the contrast between Moses and Christ, especially in places where Jesus is rejected in the name of Moses.

Before we continue our journey through the Gospel of John, let's briefly highlight a couple more things. John emphasizes that God became flesh for a particular purpose—to die. Yes, to die in order to redeem His creation. The "hour" in this Gospel is synonymous with the Cross. Throughout the narrative you may follow the development of this theme as we get closer and closer to the "hour" (see John 2:4; 7:6, 8, 30; 8:20; 12:23; 13:1; 17:1).

There is so much to discuss about John's portrait of Jesus. In this booklet, we will concentrate on some of the dialogues between Jesus and other characters in the narrative. Their lives were changed through these encounters, and I pray that ours will be also.

At the end of the narrative, the beloved disciple reveals himself as the author of the Gospel (John 21:20–25). He also says that there are so many more things to be said: "There are also many other things which Jesus did, which if they were written in detail, I suppose that even the world itself would not contain the books that would be written" (verse 25). The 3-D picture of Jesus is too wonderful, too great for words to explain. Its title is "The Word of God Became a Person. Jesus!"

Let's put on our faith glasses and see the glory of God!

The Antidote

One of the most dramatic experiences of my life happened on a Sunday afternoon, as I returned from a weekend of camping. I opened the door of my second-floor condo and placed my bag by the dining room table. That's when I saw it! A *huge* snake—right next to me, trying to climb the wall by the table. Shrieking, I instinctively jumped back without fully grasping what I was seeing—a snake in my second-floor condo in the middle of town! I ran out of my place; the snake had taken over. I called the neighbors; I called everyone. No one could give me any feasible explanation of how the snake entered my condo. The most "comforting" explanation came from the Department of Animal Control. The operator said, "Snakes travel through air-conditioning vents. This is the second time that this sort of occurrence has happened in this city in the past ten years." Small comfort! For the next twelve months, I became obsessed with checking the place for snakes. Before I got into the bed, I checked between the sheets; I looked into the bathtub, on the chairs, under the dining room table—everywhere! Snakes have a way of getting our attention, don't they? And I find it fascinating that Jesus used a snake to teach a religious man about salvation. I bet Nicodemus never forgot the snake either.

The first extended dialogue that we find in the Gospel of John takes place between Jesus and Nicodemus (John 3:1–21). In order for us to fully understand the conversation, we need to be aware that John uses the two-level narrative technique—the literal and the spiritual—that we discussed in the previous chapter. It's interesting that for his first dialogue, John chooses a member of the ruling class, a representative of "the Jews" (rulers of Pharisaic Judaism who would become hostile toward Jesus). Wouldn't you think that religious leaders and religious people have all the correct answers? Well, apparently not. Nicodemus's belief system is so inadequate that Jesus needs to totally overhaul it and shake it to its very core. If you have been frustrated with religious systems claiming to have all the answers, read on. If you have been satisfied with religious systems claiming to have all the answers, read on. We all are in desperate need to hear the snake story.

Nicodemus, the Pharisee

Nicodemus was a Pharisee and, as such, he carefully observed the law and held high the traditions of the elders. His name, though Greek, was used among the Jews. But he was no ordinary Jew; he was a ruler of the Jews, most likely a member of the Sanhedrin (John 7:45–52), the ruling council of the Jews. He kept the law, he taught the law, he interpreted the law—he seemed to have it all together. You know, like those people in church who seem to know it all, keep it all, and barely need a Savior.

Appropriately, Nicodemus comes to Jesus at night. I say "appropriately" because he is influence-conscious, and he cares for the weaker brother. He is a ruler and a teacher (see John 3:10), and therefore, he cannot publicly endorse a new colleague without asking him some questions, especially because Jesus had not attended the right schools. Interestingly enough, Jesus will conclude this dialogue discussing light and darkness. He is the Light (John 1:5; 3:18–21), and whoever does not have Him is—well, in a darker darkness than the darkest night. Even if such a person is a teacher of the law.

The diplomatic ruler opens with an impressive assertion: " 'Rabbi, we know that You have come from God . . . for no one can do these signs that You do unless God is with him' " (John 3:2). Wow! How diplomatic, Nicodemus. Curiously, he speaks in plural ("*we* know"). He represents a group, a ruling group of educated and religious people. He represents everyone who ever took the law of God seriously. And as many of us who are in that group, he is sure that he has the answers ("we know"). Except that he does not know who Jesus *really* is because he calls Him a teacher. A teacher who has come from God and is therefore a colleague. A good one. Good enough to establish a flattering dialogue with. One who performs signs during the day and invites stimulating conversations during the night.

Jesus, the Son of man

Jesus refuses to continue the courteous exchange. In the first-century world, the informal principle of reciprocity was of utmost importance and the unspoken *colleague contract* should have elicited a series of flattering comments from Jesus to Nicodemus, as part of the ongoing mutual support rooted in a sense of honor (Jesus was expected to possess social manners which honorable persons were trained to have). But Jesus always gave priority to His salvific agenda. If Nicodemus wanted instruction on salvation, Jesus was certainly going to give it to him.

Skipping the expected flattery, Jesus introduces His shattering comment with an emphatic, " 'Truly, truly, I say to you' " (verse 3). In one sentence Jesus overthrows the entire means of salvation that Nicodemus believed in. In the only passage in this Gospel that mentions the kingdom of God (verses 3 and 5), Jesus explains that whatever Nicodemus stands for is not enough for salvation. He must be born from above, with spiritual water if he is to see and enter the kingdom of God. It is helpful to notice that water is another prominent theme in this Gospel; some have claimed that a mention, or an allusion to it, may be found in every sign and dialogue in John. Jesus declares that He is the Water (John 7:37) and that the type of washing He offers, no one else can duplicate (John 13:8).

Nicodemus interprets Jesus' words as referring to a physical birth. Remember the two levels? The literal level is right before our eyes; the spiritual level is perceived only through faith in Jesus. Why would Nicodemus interpret these words in such a manner when it seems so obvious that they are pointing to a spiritual reality? Have you ever been in denial, ignoring the obvious? I certainly have. Sometimes I just didn't want to know, because if I knew, then I had to deal with the situation. Perhaps Nicodemus *chose* to misunderstand. Perhaps his dignity was at stake. The truth is that when Proselytes (circumcised non-Jews) converted to the Jewish religion, they were considered to be spiritually newborn children. So Nicodemus most likely understood the concept but couldn't accept it as truth. Jesus might have misunderstood his name. He is startled! Jesus! I am Nicodemus! You must be mistaken. Can anyone in this room tell Jesus who I am?

But no one did because no one else was there. Just Nicodemus and Jesus. At night.

Nicodemus is baffled, and his last words in this dialogue are no longer a "we know," but a "how can these things be?" Why is it so hard to understand that it is impossible to fit oneself for salvation, even though we seem to be on the right track (or in the right church)?

By now Jesus has been addressing Nicodemus in plural, perhaps sending a message to the group he represents or to the entire human race: " 'Do not be amazed that I said to you, "You [you people] must be born again" ' " (John 3:7). I guess many of us are startled when we realize that our law-keeping is not enough for salvation. I still remember where I was when the realization finally hit me. Amazed is an understatement! Shaken to the core is much more like it!

The snake story

Jesus answers Nicodemus with a reminder that he should understand these things. After all, he is " 'the teacher of Israel' " (verse 10). Some scholars believe that Jesus' usage of the definite article *the* implies that Nicodemus is more than just one of the teachers, that he holds a higher rank because he is identified as "the teacher." Nevertheless, whatever rank he might hold, it has not qualified Nicodemus to understand the things that Jesus is explaining. Jesus goes on to utter His third "Truly, truly" (verse 11; see also verses 3 and 5), now Himself speaking in first person plural: " 'We speak of what we know.' " Now the categories are *we* versus *you people*. Who are the "we"? Some propose that Jesus is talking about His disciples. However, I believe He is talking in the name of the Godhead, already introduced in John 1:1. *We* really know what *We* are saying, but *you people* don't accept *Our* testimony (see John 3:11). Keep in mind that "you people" are the law-keeping people, the churchgoers— not the Gentiles or the lawless.

Then Jesus tells the snake story. You see, Nicodemus knew the history of Israel like the back of his hand. Jesus decides to explain salvation through this story found in Numbers 21:4–9. Take a moment to read it. The people of Israel are tired and impatient. They hate the food. They hate everything. I am sure you've been there: everything is bad, the whole world is not worth it, and we say to God, "That's it! No more." In this case, God says, "OK," and removes His protection from them in the middle of the miserable desert. Venomous snakes start biting the people and many die. Israel repents. They ask Moses to intercede with Yahweh (the LORD) on their behalf. God comes up with seemingly the most ridiculous antidote to snakebites ever: " 'Make a fiery serpent, and set it on a standard [pole]; and it shall come about, that everyone who is bitten, when he looks at it, he will live' " (verse 8).

It is only natural to want to drink something or inject something to counteract the venom. This is how an antidote works. You get it into your system. But salvation in this case would happen when those who were bitten looked in faith to the bronze serpent. Salvation was outside their system, hanging on a pole. And in faith they could come to believe and understand that salvation was not within, not in their hands. Those who looked—lived.

Nicodemus! You've been bitten!

2—J.   • 17 •

Snake typology applied to Jesus

Now, Nicodemus, see if you understand salvation. Jesus is about to reveal to you the purpose of His own death as fulfillment of the snake story. It is in this narrative that the best known verse of the entire Bible is found. " 'As Moses lifted up the serpent in the wilderness, even so must the Son of Man be lifted up; so that whoever believes will in Him have eternal life. For God so loved the world, that He gave His only begotten Son, that whoever believes in Him shall not perish, but have eternal life. For God did not send the Son into the world to judge the world, but that the world might be saved through Him' " (John 3:14–17).

Jesus spoke of His death as being " 'lifted up' " (John 12:32). *Everyone* who looks at the cross and believes in Him has eternal life. *Whoever, everyone, each person* who understands that they have been bitten and then choose to look up, will live. For some reason, this truth is harder for Pharisees to understand than for anyone else. No wonder Jesus said that prostitutes and tax collectors would enter the kingdom ahead of the Pharisees (see Matthew 21:31). Tax collectors and prostitutes already know they have been bitten and need an antidote; Pharisees—not so much.

Why would Jesus identity Himself with a snake? Doesn't the serpent represent the devil, evil, and sin? Oh, yes! That's the beauty of the typology: "He made Him who knew no sin to be sin on our behalf, so that we might become the righteousness of God in Him" (2 Corinthians 5:21).

The antidote for me

You see, Nicodemus needed to understand that salvation comes from Jesus' perfect life and death on our behalf, not from our own keeping of the law. People use the word *gospel* ("good news") for many things, and it becomes confusing. The gospel is outside of us, and it happened two thousand years ago. Jesus saved the world; He is the Antidote! What the Holy Spirit does *in* us, transforming us, changing us to desire the law of God is not the gospel; it is the outcome of understanding and accepting the antidote. We have assurance of salvation because of what Christ has done *for* us. What He does *in* us is not what saves us; that's what He does after we accept His salvation. He will help us to live our lives for His glory, to attract others to His kingdom, to live healthily for our own happiness.

Nicodemus was confused. He thought that the law and tradition saved him. He didn't know that he had been bitten. That night Jesus offered him the antidote: Himself. The law reflects God's character and principles for life. We should study it. Follow it. It is good. But it does not save us. Only the Antidote does.

The snake story is a powerful symbol of the Cross. What a visual aid! I am not going to ask you to go buy a snake so that you never forget your salvation. But I do ask you to accept and appropriate the antidote for yourself. Let's read together John 3:16 very slowly, replacing *the world* and *whoever* with our own names: "For God so loved _____, that He gave His only begotten Son, that _____ [who] believes in Him shall not perish, but have eternal life." Really! It's true!

Can you imagine those bitten people in the desert? Can you imagine how they felt when they realized the antidote counteracted the venom, when they realized they wouldn't die? Wooo! Hooo! What do you think they did? Cry? Sing? Dance? Jump up and down? I bet *that* was a snake story they never forgot!

I hope this is a snake story *you* will forever remember!

The Exchange

Several years ago, I went through a very difficult time in my life. It was a time of loneliness and, in many ways, shame. Life was not working out the way I had planned, and pain filled my heart. During that time, I really needed support, but it was hard to find a safe place. My family was always there for me, loving me through it all. But I also wanted support outside of my family. I needed a place to pour out my soul, my tears, and my shattered dreams; somehow dreams die very slowly, and we all need someone to mourn with us. My life was lonely and somewhat isolated—even though it did not appear so from the outside—until God provided support, which He did through three girlfriends that I found in a self-help program. I didn't want to engage people in lengthy conversations at church; I didn't want any inquiries. If someone asked me specific questions, I gave very superficial answers. I really wanted to be *alone*—but not really. During this time, God provided for me a wonderful mentor for my emotional health, Dr. Mitch Henson, who has since passed away. Mitch, a very skilled pastor, counselor, and personal friend, walked with me on this lonely path and helped me navigate my own questions and self-discovery. One by one, he helped me shed many layers, invisible coats of hurt and frustration, under which I had hidden for a long time. Once my heart was exposed, in spirit and in truth, I underwent the most significant metamorphosis of my life. Somehow, my religious beliefs traveled the longest journey ever: thirteen inches—from my head to my heart.

Maybe this is why the story of the Samaritan woman is so dear to me. I picture her buried under layers of hurt, surviving in a hostile world by using skillful avoidance techniques. But the Person she would meet on that fateful day refused to stop probing until He got to her heart.

The wrong place at the right time

The details provided in John 4:4–6 are very revealing. Noting both the geographical location and the time of day are important in understanding the dialogue that follows. One of the first details to notice is the verb phrase that initiates this journey: "He had to pass through Samaria" (John 4:4). What does it mean He "had to pass"? Was it really necessary? At that time, everybody would know that no Jew ever had to go through Samaria. Strict Jews took a longer route so that they wouldn't have to go through Samaria. They didn't want to be "contaminated" by contact with the Samaritans.

It seems that Jesus' need to go through Samaria was spiritual—not geographical. He didn't mind being in the *wrong* place because it was the *right* time.

Why would a Jew add a few miles to his journey in order to avoid Samaria? I am so glad you asked that question! The Jews were hostile to the Samaritans after the Assyrians conquered the northern kingdom of Israel in 722 b.c. The Assyrians had an interesting method of conquering the land and its culture: they would exile some of the inhabitants to Assyria and would settle some Assyrians in the newly conquered territory. (You can read about the practice in 2 Kings 17:23–33.) This way they would blend the races and religions. The newcomers brought with them their own gods, and soon the inhabitants of the land were blending religious practices. While eventually the Samaritans worshiped only Yahweh (the God of Israel), they accepted only part of the Jewish Scriptures as sacred: the Pentateuch (the first five books of the Bible). This had created a long-standing grudge between the Jews and Samaritans, and it was the reason why the two didn't get along. This bitterness overflowed into many areas of their lives, including the location of the worship place, as we will see later in the story.

Fascinating, isn't it? Before we go on to the actual dialogue between Jesus and the Samaritan woman, we need to look at another bit of information in these introductory verses. The city of Samaria was "Sychar, near the parcel of ground that Jacob gave to his son Joseph; and Jacob's well was there" (John 4:5, 6). Sychar was a small village close to Shechem. Here we get very close to a story that you probably know well: the story of Joseph and his multicolored coat. Pause for a moment and read this fascinating story in Genesis 37. Joseph's brothers were pasturing Jacob's flocks in Shechem when Joseph went looking for them. When he arrived, he learned that they had moved the flocks to Dothan (about thirteen miles away). Shortly after Joseph located them, his brothers sold him to Midianite traders, who took him to Egypt. By the end of Jacob's life (Genesis 48:21, 22), he gave this very land to Joseph as an inheritance; Joseph was eventually buried in Shechem (Joshua 24:32). Isn't it amazing how many times our lives come full circle? We end up exactly in the place where we started, but by then we have traveled a journey that gives meaning and purpose to our lives.

Layers

A woman of Samaria came to draw water at the sixth hour, which is noon. Just as Nicodemus in John 3 came at night to avoid witnesses, this woman in John 4 comes at noon to avoid the glances of her neighbors. One of the most intriguing dialogues of the Bible is about to take place. Keep in mind that the Gospel of John is written on two levels. The conversation between Jesus and the Samaritan woman will repeatedly switch between the literal and the spiritual: the water she came to draw from the well and the Water of Life that Jesus offers. Intertwined in the two levels of dialogue are glimpses of the layers of pain and fear she tried to protect through avoidance techniques. Ssshhh! Let's listen in. Jesus is about to speak.

" 'Give Me a drink' " (John 4:7).

" 'How is it that You, being a Jew, ask me for a drink since I am a Samaritan woman?' (For Jews have no dealings with Samaritans.)" (verse 9). Yes, we know. Have you ever felt the pain of being considered a second-class citizen? Her first attempt to avoid this conversation is PREJUDICE. Maybe Jesus didn't notice that she is a Samaritan woman. She probably thinks that Jesus will stop right there! After all, He is a Jew—and a man. I am a female Latino pastor. I've heard this type of talk. But not from Jesus. He *never* speaks the language of prejudice. Instead, He offers her a gift: Please ask Me for the Living Water, Jesus says. Of the four Gospels, only here does Jesus speak in terms of a free gift. And He offers the gift to the Samaritan woman!

Sir, I don't know what you are talking about. The gift of Living Water? You don't have anything to draw with, and the well is deep. Then she uses a very powerful avoidance attempt, a layer that offers her identity and security: HERITAGE (pedigree). You see, heritage is a wonderful thing to have, to know our roots, to remember where we come from, and to understand the way God has led us in the past. But it is a terrible thing when we use our heritage to claim superiority. " 'You are not greater than our father Jacob, are You, who gave us the well, and drank of it himself and his sons and his cattle?' " (verse 12).

"Greater than your father Jacob? I AM the great I AM! Here is My business card!" That's what I would have said if I were Jesus. "I AM the God of Abraham, Isaac, and Jacob! Are you kidding Me?" I have heard that type of superiority talk also, unfortunately from my own mouth. But Jesus does not use the My-Daddy-is-bigger-than-yours type of language. He just continues His salvation agenda, leaving behind the story of Jacob and Joseph and the multicolored coat. He has one purpose and seems to ignore everything she's saying. " 'Everyone who drinks of this water will thirst again; but whoever [yes, *whoever*] drinks of the water that I will give him shall never thirst; but the water that I will give him will become in him a well of water springing up to eternal life' " (verses 13, 14).

OK, she says, I give up. Give me that water and let's get it over with. At least I won't have to come to the well anymore—especially not at noon.

Well, says Jesus, I am glad that you stopped by to discuss race and religious background. Now let's get personal; let's talk about you. After all, *you* are the reason why I *had* to pass through Samaria! " 'Go, call your husband and come here' " (verse 16). Simple request, isn't it?

Simple answer: I have no husband. Was it really true? Yes, sort of.

I used to have a master's degree in the third layer: SUPERFICIAL TRUTH. Minimizing, justifying, and denying are effective avoidance techniques. Who wants to tell the truth and nothing but the truth under the circumstances? Who wants to engage in lengthy conversations with church members? Who wants to share that you just spent the whole night crying because your kid is in jail or you feel rejected by your husband? So, you come to church late so no one can have a chance to ask. And, if someone does approach you with a "How are you today?" you know how to say a fake but lighthearted "Fine, thank you, and you?" Many dream of the time when we all will feel so safe at church that at a time like this we would be able to answer, "Not good. Really not good, and let me tell you why . . ."

Impressive, Jesus said. You are telling the truth. " 'You have had five husbands, and the one whom you now have is not your husband; this you have said truly' " (verse 18). I would pay a million dollars (which I don't have) to see the body language of the Samaritan woman during Jesus' reply recorded in verses 18 and 19. Her jaw must have dropped! Her eyes opened wide! Heart racing and palms sweating, trying to imagine who could have possibly told this Man all these things. The naked reality of her life was buried under all these layers of avoidance. Who had opened the closet? Her skeletons were roaming around! Watch out!

The painful truth is out. In an age when only men had the prerogative to initiate divorce, she had been rejected five times, and the man she is with now does not even have the decency of offering her the umbrella of his kinship in formal marriage. He just sleeps with her. No wonder that she feels rejected—by men—by society. But not by Jesus.

These revelations of Jesus must have been very hard for her to hear because now she resorts to the most powerful avoidance attempt in the entire narrative. This Stranger has just demonstrated that He can read her past like an open book. I mean, He really knows her past! She could ask for anything she wants—advice, insight, hope. So, she chooses the subject: mountains! What? Yes, she says, let's not talk about me; let's talk about mountains. This layer is called RELIGIOSITY, a preoccupation with rules and regulations. It is one of the most effective ways to block the gospel of Jesus Christ from coming into our hearts. As long as I am focusing on religious stuff, such as the right mountain to worship on, the manner and style of worship in church, or even the color of the carpet in the sanctuary—well, you get the picture. I'm OK as long as we are not talking about me! Who wants to talk about me anyway? It sure smells bad in the closet where all the skeletons are. "The woman said to Him, 'Sir, I perceive that You are a prophet. Our fathers worshiped in this mountain, and you people say that in Jerusalem is the place where men ought to worship' " (verses 19, 20). The fact is that the place of worship had been the cause of a long-lasting quarrel between Jews and Samaritans. When the Jews started to rebuild the temple after the Babylonian exile, the Samaritans offered to help. But the Jews refused their offer (Ezra 4:2, 3). Then the Samaritans built their own temple on Mount Gerizim around 400 B.C. The Jews destroyed the Samaritan temple in 128 B.C. The Samaritans obviously were not too happy about it, and so it went—you get the point.

Jesus' response to religiosity continues to be the same now as it was then: " 'An hour is coming, and now is, when the true worshipers will worship the Father in spirit and truth. . . . Those who worship Him must worship in spirit and truth' " (John 4:23, 24). Oh, yes! The Father delights in those worshipers who worship Him anywhere, anytime, any way from the heart and with transparency of soul. God is a God of people, not of places as were the other "gods" in ancient times. He is where we are. So let's worship Him! But we carry so many layers of hurt, don't we?

Then the woman used the last layer of avoidance she had left—PROCRASTINATION. OK, Sir, I don't have to deal with this right now. The Messiah is coming, and then He will clarify all these things. I will deal with it then.

Little does she know that she is about to hear what no one has ever heard before.

The exchange

If I were this woman, by now I would be feeling pretty vulnerable. She had used everything she had—all her defenses—but this Man, whoever He was, was still there. She was not used to that. Every man who had known her well, had left her. Not this One. But she went from feeling vulnerable and curious to being absolutely shocked. To her statement about a coming Messiah, Jesus responded, " 'I who speak to you am He' " (verse 26). Can you imagine? I AM the great I AM, the Coming One, and I have been speaking to *you* all this time. This is the only place in all four Gospels, where Jesus admits, before His trial, that He is the Messiah. And this revelation, never before heard in the first person singular, is given to this Samaritan woman.

Then something amazing happens. "The woman left her waterpot" (verse 28). She left her waterpot! The very same pot she had brought to draw water with, heavy with layers of hurt and fear! She left her waterpot! She had taken a sip of the Living Water, and water from the well didn't matter anymore. She had exchanged her water for His water, and she could not stop the overflow! The narrative in verse 28 says that she went to the city—the same woman who didn't like crowds and neighbors' glances—and spoke to the men (maybe she knew them better than the women, but the Greek word can also mean a "human being" or a "person").

Her testimony is *striking.* He has " 'told me all the things that I have done' " (verses 29, 39). He knows everything about me, and He is still talking to me! Could this be the Christ? Is it possible that Someone can know me fully, intimately, and still love me? Many of us have sought an answer for that question. She found the answer. She had made the exchange. She was ready to leave her waterpot and drink of His water. The layers had been shed; she was ready for more Living Water. She became the most successful evangelist in all the Gospels. Many of the Samaritans believed in Jesus (see verses 39–42). They even called Jesus " 'the Savior of the world' " (verse 42). In all of the New Testament, this title for Jesus is found only here and in 1 John 4:14. How is that for a metamorphosis? That is what the Living Water does to you.

Leaving our waterpots

The gospel of Jesus Christ is the great exchange. We have life through His death.

> *He* was pierced through for *our* transgressions,
> *He* was crushed for *our* iniquities;
> The chastening for *our* well-being fell upon *Him,*
> And by *His* scourging *we* are healed (Isaiah 53:5; emphasis added).

Take a moment to look at the pronouns in this passage. See all the terms *He, Him,* and *His* and all the terms *we* and *our*? He not only paid for our iniquities and transgressions; He also purchased our well-being and healing. We leave our waterpots; He gives us His eternal life.

Many years ago, I attended a Christmas party to which everyone was to bring a gift for a gift exchange. Numbers were drawn and we played in order. We could choose a wrapped gift or exchange it for one that someone else had already opened. A young man was very excited to open his gift—until he saw what was inside. It was a showerhead. Most of us adults could envision a hot-massaging shower, but not this teenager. His face was downcast. On the other hand, one of the adults got a really cool tool. When the party was over, I saw that adult approach the teenager and offer him a trade—and the expression on the teen's face totally changed.

Like at that gift exchange, Jesus offers us a better trade. You see, Jesus showed up at the party with eternal life; we showed up with death. At the end of the evening, we left with Jesus' eternal life, and He left with our death sentence and died on the cross (see Romans 3:23–26). That's the great exchange, the gospel of Jesus Christ.

I want to invite you to leave your waterpot. Trade your sorrows, your past, your hurt, your layers, the skeletons in your closet, your shame, and your loneliness. He already paid for all that and, in addition, purchased your healing. Do a little ceremony with God. Choose a small waterpot or a stone or something that you can throw on the floor. Symbolically, place your hands on that object, transferring to it all the layers of shame that you have been living with, and then pray for forgiveness, peace, and freedom in His name. Then let go. Never again question whether you should carry this weight. He is faithful to forgive (see 1 John 1:9). Accept His living water, and you will become free to be the person you were meant to be.

Isn't it interesting that the Bible ends with this invitation? "The Spirit and the bride say, 'Come.' And let the one who hears say, 'Come.' And let the one who is thirsty come; let the one who wishes take the water of life without cost" (Revelation 22:17).

Oh, yes! Did I mention it before? Without cost—for us. It cost Jesus His life.

And now—for you, it is a gift!

The Verdict

When I was a little girl, my parents took me to the city of Córdoba in Argentina. My father, then a pastor, would be attending workers' meetings in a hotel for a few days. My mother anticipated a good time in the company of other pastors' wives, and we, the children, excitedly looked forward to spending every minute of the day playing in the hotel's swimming pool. I was three, and I was told in no uncertain terms that I was to stay in the shallow part of the pool at all times, no exceptions! The happy day finally arrived, and I found myself in water bliss. I was obedient to my parents' instructions, as usual. (My mother would probably interject a correction at this point to set the record straight.) But suddenly, I found myself in water at the edge of the forbidden zone, and the bottom of the pool was very slippery. Very slippery! Green and slimy. I started sliding toward the deep end of the pool as if I were in an underwater playground—except that this was no fun. I found myself in the very place where my mother told me not to go; and now I knew, in my young three-year-old heart, that I would die because I had no way out.

But there was something else that my heart knew; if my mother saw me, she would rescue me. Somehow in my young brain, I understood that my mother's love for me would oblige her to jump in and save me. But the problem was that she couldn't see me! I gathered all my strength and tried to jump up, pushing my feet against the bottom of the pool, but I was already under the water and only my hand would briefly appear above the surface and then disappear again. I tried it again and again—and my mother saw me! Yes, she noticed my little fingers above the water and that was all she needed. She dove into the pool! It didn't matter what she was wearing and who was watching. All that mattered to her was that her little girl was drowning and she had to save her. And she did save me! My mother didn't need to consult a parenting textbook to learn what to do in such circumstances. Her mother's instinct and love made her do what a mother does best: save her child!

In this chapter, we will study the story of a woman who ended up exactly where she was told not to go—the deep end of the pool. And she was sure she would die because there was no way out. That is, until Jesus showed up and changed the direction of the story.

The court

During the first century A.D., this story, found in John 8:2–11, circulated in the early church on its own, not attached to other narratives. Though it is absent from the earliest manuscripts, the story is found in later manuscripts, sometimes elsewhere, for example at the end of Luke 21 and at the end of the Gospel of John. Most of the stories about Jesus circulated on their own during the period of oral traditions, when the followers of Jesus preserved the accounts, parables, sayings, miracles, and dialogues of Jesus through the word of mouth. Eventually, these oral traditions made their way into the written form. For several reasons, I like the placement of this story in our current versions of the Bible in this particular spot. First, it is significant that John's eighth chapter begins with the adulterous woman's accusers suggesting that she should be stoned to death, and it ends with the Jews picking up stones to throw them at Jesus (verse 59). Furthermore, in this chapter the woman who was supposed to be condemned is set free, while the Jews, who don't believe they need to be set free, end up rejecting the only real Source of freedom: " 'If the Son makes you free, you will be free indeed' " (verse 36), and thereby condemn themselves. I also find fascinating the fact that this story fits perfectly in the series of stories that seem to contrast Moses with Jesus, as if one had to decide to either be a disciple of Moses or a disciple of Jesus (see John 6:30–

58; 7:19–24; 9). Finally, in the following chapter (John 9:28, 29), the Pharisees proclaim themselves disciples of Moses and reject Jesus because of His manner of Sabbath keeping (something interesting to think about).

The story takes place in the temple: "Early in the morning He came again into the temple, and all the people were coming to Him; and He sat down and began to teach them" (John 8:2). The scribes and Pharisees in the narrative appear eager to humiliate this woman, caught in adultery. They could have kept her in custody elsewhere while speaking with Jesus. But they really want to make an example out of her, and so they take her to the center of the temple court where everyone can see her (see verse 3). Now the court of the temple becomes a court of law, as the accusers bring a legal question to Jesus. It was a routine procedure to take such cases to a rabbi for a decision. But Jesus was no ordinary rabbi.

The charge

The charge against this woman is clear: *adultery.* The Jewish law required witnesses in order to make such charge; therefore, the narrative clearly states that this woman was caught "in the very act" (verse 4). Adultery was one of the three gravest sins for Jews; they would rather die than find themselves caught in idolatry, murder, or adultery. Next, the scribes and the Pharisees refer to the Law of Moses: " 'Now in the Law Moses commanded us to stone such women; what then do You say?' " (verse 5). Interesting, isn't it? When was the last time you came to church with the Bible in one hand and stones in the other? I know of churches where it happens. I hope not in yours.

Two passages in the Pentateuch deal with such laws: Leviticus 20:10 and Deuteronomy 22:22–24. Leviticus 20:10 states, " ' "If there is a man who commits adultery with another man's wife, one who commits adultery with his friend's wife, the adulterer and the adulteress shall surely be put to death." ' " In this instance, if a man has sexual relations with the wife of a neighbor, both shall be put to death. The method is not identified. The law in Deuteronomy 22 states that " 'if there is a girl who is a virgin engaged to a man, and another man finds her in the city and lies with her, then you shall bring them both out to the gate of that city and you shall stone them to death' " (verses 23, 24). The Law of Moses required stoning *only* when the girl was a virgin engaged to be married. There is no mention of such being the case; neither is there a man present to receive the death penalty also; and this is not taking place at the gate of the city. There is no doubt that the scribes and the Pharisees are manipulating the law a bit. The narrative tells us that their motive is to test Jesus "so that they might have grounds for accusing Him" (verse 6). But the truth is, apart from all the excuses and manipulations of her accusers, that the woman is GUILTY!

Have you ever been guilty of something that you knew was wrong and then felt condemned by the law? Adultery, abortion, pride, stealing, murder of the body or the soul, bad parenting, lying, self-righteousness, and so forth? I am sure you have. If you think you haven't, well—John says you are making God a liar. (Sorry to put it that way, but it is in the Bible, right there in 1 John 1:10.) So, now that you and I know that we are all as guilty as was the adulterous woman, let's place ourselves right beside her, in the center of the court, condemned and without a way out, knowing that we deserve to die. "All have sinned and fall short of the glory of God" (Romans 3:23). So, are you there in the center of the court? If you are, continue reading. Now you are ready to experience what the adulterous woman experienced that day. Only those who understand the bad news can rejoice with the good news!

Verdict: Guilty!

So, there is Jesus. The trap is cleverly set. The dilemma is this: the Jews had no power to carry out a death sentence under the Roman law (John 18:31). So, if Jesus said, "Go ahead! Stone her!" then they could go to the Roman authorities and make a charge against Jesus. If Jesus said, "No! Leave her alone!" then He would be teaching them to break the Law of Moses and would be discredited as a rabbi. Pretty clever trap, isn't it?

Jesus wrote something on the ground (John 8:6). This is the only time recorded in all four Gospels that Jesus wrote anything. I wish the narrative told us what He wrote! But it doesn't. A suggestion emerges from later manuscripts that add that He wrote the sins of each one of them. This claim could be substantiated by the fact that the Greek word for "to write" is *graphō* and John 8:6 uses *katagraphō,* which can mean "to write down a record against someone" because one of the meanings of *kata* is "against" (it can also mean "wrote down" because He was writing on the ground). Whatever the case may be, the verdict is clear: " 'He who is without sin among you, let him be the first to throw a stone at her' " (verse 7).

Can you feel the intensity of the moment, right there in the center of the court? Are you afraid? Are you covering your head? How *do* you prepare to be stoned? By the way, there was a news piece a few weeks ago about the stoning of an adulterous man somewhere in Africa. They buried him in the ground, leaving only his shoulders and head exposed—terrible even to think about it; he couldn't even use his hands to cover his face!

Jesus simply specified those who were qualified to carry out the sentence—those who were without sin or sinful desires. These legal experts were conscience stricken and began to leave one by one while Jesus was still writing on the ground (verses 8 and 9). No one was qualified. No one! No—wait. One did qualify! "He was left alone, and the woman, where she was, in the center of the court" (verse 9).

By His own definition, Jesus was the only One who could throw the stones! Get ready! The stones are coming! We are about to die! We deserve it!

The sentence carried out

"Jesus said to her, 'Woman, where are they? Did no one condemn you?' She said, 'No one, Lord.' And Jesus said, 'I do not condemn you, either. Go. From now on sin no more' " (verses 10, 11). What? Not condemned? What do you mean? How dare Jesus do that? Does He not care about the law? Isn't the finger that wrote on the ground the same finger that wrote the law?

Well, this is why the Gospel of John was written—so that we might understand what Jesus really did for us. You see, Jesus aborted this stoning, and, a few days later, the only One who was qualified to throw the stone, did throw the stone. But He threw the stone on Himself, and in doing so He took the penalty that she deserved. That we all deserve.

When Jesus was hanging on the cross, John records Him as saying, " 'It is finished!' " (John 19:30). What was finished? All condemnation for those who believe in Jesus was finished because the sinless Son of God took humanity's death penalty upon Himself. The entire sacrificial system of the Jewish Scriptures was pointing to this very moment. No wonder that in the first chapter of this Gospel (verse 29), Jesus is introduced as " 'the Lamb of God who takes away the sin of the world!' "

Jesus always speaks to us in the same order. First, "I do not condemn you"; then, "Go. . . . Sin no more." God wants us to live healthier lives for His glory and for our happiness, but He never reverses the order. He never says, "Sin no more, and then I won't condemn you." He has already paid our death penalty on the cross. John is very specific about the purpose of God becoming flesh: " 'God did not send the Son into the world to judge the world, but that the world might be saved through Him' " (John 3:17).

Jesus jumped in the pool. And He saved us.

There are many days, sometimes weeks, months, and years, when we feel condemned, guilty as charged. Sometimes, other people condemn us; sometimes, we condemn ourselves. Guilt is heavy, and it disables us by not allowing us to become who God has designed us to be. I urge you, in the name of Jesus Christ, to be free today.

This visualization might be useful to you: sit on the floor and close your eyes; imagine yourself in the center of the court. You know you are guilty. Perhaps no one else knows. Listen to the charge that you deserve to die: this is the bad news. Now confess your sin and claim Jesus' blood on your behalf. Then listen to Jesus' response to you: "I don't condemn you; go and sin no more." This is the good news. Believe what He is saying. Really! It is true! "If the Son makes you free, you will be free indeed" (John 8:36). Leave your burden at the foot of the cross. Get up from the ground, and go on to live a life for God's glory to the full potential that His Spirit enables you. From caterpillar to butterfly.

Now let's rejoice with the apostle Paul. Read these words aloud, and place your name in the blank: "Therefore there is now no condemnation for _____ who [is] in Christ Jesus" (Romans 8:1). Feel lighter? After all, you already know the end of your story—your sins have been cast away from you as far as the east is from the west (see Psalm 103:12).

How far is the east from the west?

Really? Wooo! Hooo!

The Light

Have you ever seen before-and-after commercials? These commercials, used in a variety of industries (such as weight loss, dentistry, cosmetic surgery, etc.), highlight the way a person looked before the procedure or program and after it. Well, in this chapter, we will analyze my favorite before-and-after story. A man born blind, who sits begging every day, is touched by Jesus. And when the Light gets a hold of him, it changes his life completely. He becomes a bold witness for Jesus, and we can barely recognize that he is the same man. I love this story! It is the epitome of the caterpillar-to-butterfly story. On the other hand, this story makes me sad. It reminds me of my days as a Pharisee, when I used to impose my interpretations of how to keep the law on everyone else. And I feel exposed by this narrative. But the good news is that one day the Light got a hold of me, too, and my fear was turned to joy!

The Light of the world

From the beginning of the Gospel of John, Jesus has been introduced as the "Light." Jesus is the Light of men (John 1:4, 5), exposing darkness by His very presence (John 3:19–21). In one of His "I AM" statements found in this Gospel, Jesus boldly claims, " 'I am the Light of the world; he who follows Me will not walk in the darkness, but will have the Light of life' " (John 8:12).

It is not surprising, then, that in the story of the man born blind, Jesus reminds His disciples that He is, in fact, the Light of the world. It's surprising that He does it in response to a question that follows an assumption. The disciples are sure (as many of us are in our own religious beliefs) that they know what is going on. It is obvious to them that this man's congenital blindness is the punishment for sin (it appears that some rabbis would have even entertained the idea of an infant sinning in the womb). But whose sin? "And His disciples asked Him, 'Rabbi, who sinned, this man or his parents, that he would be born blind?' " (John 9:2). Jesus addresses both their question and their assumption; they have it all wrong. There is a purpose for the blindness: " 'That the works of God might be displayed in him' " (verse 3). All the *signs* in this Gospel give glory to Jesus, as introduced in the very beginning. "We saw His glory, glory as of the only begotten from the Father, full of grace and truth" (John 1:14). So, Jesus says, the night is coming when the Light will be withdrawn from the world and it will be night (John 9:4). But for now, " 'While I am in the world, I am the Light of the world' " (verse 5). The miracle that follows this dialogue is an enacted parable of Jesus' ministry as the Light of the world. As in the other instances, every "I AM" of Jesus reveals more of who He really is.

In his typical style, John narrates this discourse on two levels: darkness and blindness, and light and sight, both literal and spiritual. It is fascinating! So, are you ready to see?

The progression

Jesus made clay and applied it to the blind man's eyes and sent the man to the pool of Siloam to wash his eyes (verses 6, 7). The man "went away and washed, and came back seeing" (verse 7). The miracle itself is only the beginning of the story, not the climax of the narrative. Please take a moment to read the entire story in John 9, and then we will continue analyzing it.

Finished? OK, let's continue. Two progressions follow the miracle. The blind man moves toward spiritual sight, while the Jewish officials descend into spiritual darkness. The author signals the progression through the different names and characteristics assigned to Jesus, both by the blind man and by the Pharisees.

The man looks so different after he received his sight that his neighbors don't fully recognize him. They think this man looks like the beggar they knew, but they are not sure. He tells them that he is, in fact, the same man (verses 8, 9). He was a beggar because it was the only way for a blind man to make a living. Now the neighbors are really intrigued! So they ask, How is it that you now see? (verse 10). He tells them the story of a man called Jesus.

Isn't it amazing how Jesus changes lives? Sometimes we wish we could see more healing miracles, but the greatest miracle happens in the hearts of those who accept Jesus as their Savior and Lord. Perhaps you are one of them. Your greatest witness is your own story and how it changed when you heard the story of Jesus. Tell how the story of Jesus changed your story! Perhaps you are on a journey, like the blind man.

Let's continue the narrative.

The blind man tells what happened; he relates the miracle of how he received sight. Note that he calls Jesus " 'the man' " (verse 11). This is where the progression starts. He has received physical sight, but his spiritual sight is only beginning, and he is progressing toward the Light. Later on, he calls Jesus " 'a prophet' " (verse 17); then he talks about Jesus as Someone worthy to be followed (verses 27, 28). Later, he boldly states that Jesus is from God (verse 33), and eventually, he understands that Jesus is the Son of man and he worships Him (verses 35–38). The Pharisees, on the other hand, are also in a progression, but toward darkness because they reject Jesus. The Pharisees start by being confused; some state that Jesus is not from God because He has healed the blind man on the Sabbath, while others wonder how a Man who could do such *signs* could also be a sinner (verse 16). They are divided—confused and doubtful. There is no problem with doubts. The problem happens when the Light given is rejected. Following their confusion, they question and challenge the miracle; they don't believe because they can't explain it according to their understanding of Sabbath keeping. Later, they call Jesus a sinner (verse 24). They end up rejecting Jesus in the name of being followers of Moses (verses 28, 29).

THE LIGHT

Are you on a journey? Do you have doubts? Are you confused? Questioning is good when it moves us to renewed faith. For instance, when we question our own interpretation of the Bible because we are seeking to know Jesus Christ better, then we are moving toward the Light. But questioning is dangerous when it prompts us to give up on God and leads us into a progression of cynicism, sarcasm, and disbelief as we descend into darkness. However, God will continue His pursuit of us. He doesn't give up on us even when we give up on Him.

Sabbath versus Jesus

This has to be one of the most paradoxical stories in all four Gospels! Jesus will be rejected in the name of the Sabbath! Yes, the " 'Lord of the Sabbath' " (Matthew 12:8) will be rejected because He didn't keep the Sabbath appropriately! Can you believe it? It reminds me of how shocked I felt when I heard the story of Charlie Chaplin anonymously entering a Chaplin look-alike contest and coming out third! What a paradox! Jesus is our Sabbath! How could He possibly breach the Sabbath?

But let's continue with our story. The neighbors take the once-blind man to the Pharisees (John 9:13). This is when the reader learns that it was the Sabbath. A legal issue is introduced. To the Pharisees, Jesus obviously breaks the Sabbath; He heals and does additional things that are not allowed on the Sabbath and even tells other people to do forbidden things also. Well, in their own interpretation of the law, that was an offense. For example, it was strictly forbidden to make clay or to wash in the pool on Sabbath. And not only that! This was a repeat offense (John 5:1–17).

The blind man now gives his second testimony of how he was healed; it's simple and it's powerful. This is his story, and he's sticking to it. " 'He applied clay to my eyes, and I washed, and I see' " (John 9:15). Then the division occurs among the Pharisees. Some focus on the apparent breaking of the Sabbath law. Others concentrate on the magnitude of the " *'signs'* " (plural) that Jesus is performing (verse

16). Jesus seems to be a sinner to them according to their understanding of Sabbath keeping. The Pharisees are the experts. Is their long-accepted interpretation of the Sabbath law being called for a re-examination? The tradition of oral law transmitted in the rabbinical schools, was held to have come from Moses (including all the details on how to keep the Sabbath). On the other hand, the *signs* performed by Jesus could not have come from a sinner. What is going on? They are so perplexed that they even ask the blind man for his opinion—not a common custom among interpreters of religion. The healed man gives Jesus the highest place he knows for a Man of God: " 'He is a prophet' " (verse 17). Interesting, isn't it? He came to the same conclusion that the Samaritan woman did (John 4:19). Of course, Jesus is a lot more than a prophet, and both the blind man and the Samaritan woman receive greater revelations from Jesus Himself. They are in the progression toward the Light.

The Pharisees? Not so. They can't explain the paradox, so they decide to discredit the miracle. There must be a flaw. Perhaps the man was not blind after all.

"The Jews" (a name commonly given to Jesus' opposition in this Gospel) called the parents of the once-blind man and questioned them: " 'Is this your son, who you say was born blind? Then how does he now see?' " (John 9:18, 19). We are told that the parents were afraid because "the Jews had already agreed that if anyone confessed" that Jesus was the awaited Christ "he was to be put out of the synagogue" (verse 22). Fear is such a paralyzing feeling, especially when it is exerted by those who seem to be the brokers of the grace of God. So, the parents stick to the facts. We only know two things: he " 'is our son, and that he was born blind,' " they reply (verse 20). But then they completely distance themselves from the miracle by their choice of pronouns: *we* and *he/him.* " 'How *he* now sees, *we* do not know; or who opened *his* eyes, *we* do not know. Ask *him; he* is of age, *he* will speak for *himself* ' " (verse 21; emphasis added). In other words, we are out of here. We don't know anything, we didn't see anything, we are not casting our vote on anyone, and we are not incriminated by this miracle. We are washing our hands from this healing. Ask him.

Disciples of Jesus or disciples of Moses?

In the final part of the narrative, both sides become increasingly bold and polarized—the Jews against Jesus and the once-blind man for Him. The blind man is called in again to share his story one more time; this is the third time already. The ones leading the interrogation begin by saying, " 'We know that this man is a sinner' " (verse 24). The *we* is emphatic: we, the religious leaders, know. The man, in turn, answers with an indisputable argument: " 'Whether He is a sinner, I do not know; one thing I do know, that though I was blind, now I see' " (verse 25). The man does not know as much as the religious leaders claim to know. He knows only one thing—that he can *see* because of Jesus. Many things may be important; only one is necessary—to know Him (see Luke 10:42). Then they ask him to tell his story again (John 9:26)! This is where the Gospel narrative becomes clearly ironic (one of the characteristics in many dialogues in the Gospel of John).

The formerly blind man answers, " 'I told you already and you did not listen; why do you want to hear it again? You do not want to become His disciples too, do you?' " (verse 27). Wow! He does not seem like an ex-beggar anymore; he is bold and his argument is flawless. Two important truths come out in his response: the Pharisees' motives are being revealed and the fact that the ex-blind man has become a disciple of Jesus, which becomes obvious when he adds the word *too*. He is definitely counting himself as a disciple of Jesus!

This is too much for the religious authorities! They are exposed and they don't like it! So the Jews state clearly that their "one thing" is not the same as the blind man's "one thing." " 'You are His disciple, but we are disciples of Moses. We know that God has spoken to Moses, but as for this man, we do not know where He is from' " (verses 28, 29). Your one thing is Jesus, they say; our one thing is Moses. John had already revealed to his readers where Jesus comes from. He comes from God and He is the full revelation of God (John 1:1, 14). Furthermore, we have already been told that Jesus is not against Moses. Moses received the law—a great revelation of God. But Jesus is greater than Moses because through Him salvation is achieved, and He is the fullest revelation of the Father: "The Law was given through Moses; grace and truth were realized through Jesus Christ" (John 1:17). But the Pharisees then, and even now, seem to think that one must choose Moses over Jesus.

"I am casting my lot with Jesus," says the blind man, and he adds, "And I find it hard to believe that you, the religion experts, can't figure out such an obvious thing as this one. That's amazing to me" (John 9:30–33; author paraphrase).

What is your "one thing"?

Real sight and real blindness

Finally, they've had it! The Jews answered the blind man, " 'You were born entirely in sins, and are you teaching us?' " (verse 34). In other words, we are the religious people and you know nothing—how dare you argue with us! Interestingly, the narrative points back to the very beginning of the story, where the disciples, not only the Jews, thought that the blindness was due to sin (verse 2). The reader already knows that the blindness occurred for the glory of God (verse 3), but the Pharisees don't seem to realize it. They put the man out of the synagogue (verse 34). The conversation is over. Or is it?

The conclusion of the narrative is the climax of the story. The results of both progressions are revealed. First is the blind man's progression. Jesus finds him and asks him if he believes in the Son of man. The ex-blind man answers with a question: " 'Who is He, Lord, that I may believe in Him?' " (verse 36). The man has only heard the voice of Jesus, but he has not seen Him because when he received sight, Jesus was no longer there. Jesus now reveals Himself fully to this excommunicated ex-beggar: " 'You have both seen Him, and He is the one who is talking with you' " (verse 37). At that moment, the once physically blind man receives complete spiritual sight. He realizes that Jesus is Someone to be worshiped. He believes in Him. I love the fact that Jesus responds, "You have . . . *seen* Him." Wooo! Hooo! Yes, both literally *and* spiritually. This is the climax! This man has seen Jesus, believed in Him, and is now worshiping Him. This is the only place in this Gospel where anyone is said to have worshiped Jesus. Wow! Talk about real sight!

On the other hand, spiritual blindness is also revealed. Jesus says something quite strange: " 'For judgment I came into this world, so that those who do not see may see, and that those who see may become blind' " (verse 39). Remember that this entire Gospel is written in two levels—the one that meets the eye, and the other involving spiritual realities that can be accessed only through believing in Jesus. So did Jesus come for judgment? Didn't we discuss it, when we looked at His dialogue with Nicodemus, that He came to save and not to judge? (see John 3:17). Well, even there Jesus explains that the very presence of Light exposes the darkness of unbelief: " 'God did not send the Son into the world to judge the world, but that the world might be saved through Him. He who believes in Him is not judged; he who does not believe has been judged already, because he has not believed in the name of the only begotten Son of God. This is the judgment, that the Light has come into the world, and men loved the darkness rather than the Light' " (John 3:17–19).

Judgment is not the purpose of the Light. That is clear. But it is a consequence of rejecting the Light. When the Pharisees heard Jesus' words on the blind seeing and the seeing ones becoming blind (John 9:39), they thought that they, of all people, could not possibly be blind. They ask, " 'We are not blind too, are we?' " (verse 40). Then Jesus says, " 'If you were blind, you would have no sin; but since you say, "We see," your sin remains' " (verse 41). Read my lips, says Jesus: You think you know and you say you know; and you say that others don't know. If you were blind, you could seek the Light. But you think you don't need the Light; therefore, the Light judges you by its very presence. I am the Light of the world! And you rejected Me.

Amazing grace

This is a piercing story to read—paradoxical dialogues, opposite progressions, exposed motives, and ironic conclusions. In the past, I felt chastised by this very story regarding my own religious arrogance. Now I know that there are many things that I don't know. But I have seen a glimpse of the Light, and I am following it with all my soul, my heart, and my mind. His amazing grace has captured me, and that's my story, the only one I have—and I am sticking to it! This is the *one thing* I do know, so well expressed by John Newton, the converted slave trader. Please sing it with me wherever you are.

> Amazing grace! how sweet the sound,
> That saved a wretch like me!
> I once was lost, but now am found,
> *Was blind, but now I see!!!*

The Life

"Unseen Certainties" is the title of a sermon I preach based on this story. It sounds like an oxymoron, doesn't it? How can you possibly be certain of that which you can't see? But this is exactly the premise on which the Gospel of John is written. There is a reality that we see, but there is a deeper and more important reality that we do not see, one that we can access only through belief in Jesus Christ. Faith is like a pair of glasses through which we contemplate an unseen reality that we come to trust above and beyond anything our physical eyes can see. Have you ever needed a pair of glasses to see clearly? I need my "faith-in-Jesus" glasses every day. I can't imagine going through life without them. We all face problems and seemingly impossible situations every day: sickness, financial problems, loneliness, relationship difficulties, death of a loved one, waiting for a difficult decision, finding a new job, and the list goes on. Without the faith glasses, we live lives of anxiety and desperation. Jesus, on the other hand, offers a life of rest and inner peace, even in the midst of trouble.

This chapter relates the seventh and last sign in this Gospel. It is the climactic sign; it is also the event that will prompt "the Jews" to plot Jesus' death. This sign also serves as a preview of Jesus' own resurrection at the end of this Gospel. *Signs* in the Gospel of John are testimonies of who Jesus really is, highlighted several times with "I AM" statements that reveal new dimensions of Jesus' ministry. In many ways this event is a summary of the Gospel's major themes; the sign performed is the raising of a dead man to life. This sign is accompanied by much publicity, being that Bethany is less than two miles from Jerusalem. The Jews are present, and this is the drop that overflows the religious leaders' cup of patience, prompting them to their final act against Jesus. Furthermore, this story contains a climactic "I AM" from Jesus, highlighting the importance of the unseen reality, accessible only through faith in Him. We will concentrate on the dialogue between Jesus and Martha who, even though willing, is having a hard time putting on those glasses of faith. But when she does, she truly beholds the glory of the Son of God. So, let's put those glasses on and get ready for an incredible outcome!

The delay

Lazarus, Martha, and Mary are introduced in the very first verse of John 11. It is interesting to notice that Mary is introduced as the one "who anointed the Lord with ointment, and wiped His feet with her hair" (verse 2). This event has not yet been narrated in this Gospel; it actually comes up in the next chapter (John 12:1–8). But it seems that John's audience is familiar with this event and the anointing by Mary is used as a point of reference to clarify Lazarus's identity.

The sisters send a message to Jesus with the news that their brother is sick. No request is made, but I think that it is safe to assume that a plea for help is implied. "So the sisters sent word to Him, saying, 'Lord, behold, he whom You love is sick' " (John 11:3). The sisters are relying on Jesus' love for Lazarus. The name *Lazarus* is a form of the name *Eleazar,* which means "God is my help." And they really need God's help at this time. They trust Jesus to do something about it: He is resourceful, He has healed people, and He has a special connection with God. They are sure He will do something for the one He loves.

When Jesus hears the news, He tells those who are with Him that there is a plan. Wouldn't you like to know the plan? This particular " 'sickness is not to end in death, but for the glory of God, so that the Son of God may be glorified by it' " (verse 4). Not to end in death? Well, then there is no problem. All the signs in this Gospel have revealed and glorified Jesus so that we may see His glory (John

1:14). There is a plan. But it is not the plan that anyone in this story imagined—not the disciples, not the sisters, nor the Jews. No one imagined what God had in mind. And the truth is, we usually don't know the plan. Only God does. And He usually does not tell. The reason for this sickness is similar to the case of the man born blind (John 9). The utmost glory of Jesus is at the Cross, and this event will lead to it. There is no other way to glory than through the Cross.

The juxtaposition of the next two verses is paradoxical: "Now Jesus loved Martha and her sister and Lazarus. So when He heard that he was sick, He then stayed two days longer in the place where He was" (John 11:5, 6). How strange! It doesn't make sense to say, "He loved—so He delayed." Or does it? Obviously, it isn't the lack of affection that delayed the Son of God. So what was it? I have come to trust God's timing even though I usually don't understand it. I have a motto that has helped me countless times: "Delays are designed to show the magnitude of the miracle." Do you like the motto? Copy it somewhere. When we can't understand God's timing, we can trust His love. Faith over fear. Faith glasses on, everybody!

Sweet sleep

Finally, Jesus tells His disciples, " 'Let us go to Judea again' " (verse 7). Again? Are You sure, Jesus? His disciples remind Him that the Jews were seeking to stone Him (see John 10:31, 39) and so they wonder, " 'Are You going there again?' " (John 11:8). They addressed Jesus as "Rabbi" in this verse for the last time in this Gospel. His public ministry is coming to an end, and His disciples seem to realize that Jesus is in imminent danger.

As was the case in the miracle of the man born blind, Jesus starts talking about day and light, and night and darkness. The night is the absence of Jesus because He is the Light of the world. It is still day—but not for long.

Jesus then explains to His disciples that " 'Lazarus has fallen asleep' " (verse 11). As it is common in this Gospel, they misunderstand what He is saying. So they respond to the literal words that they hear. OK, then, if he is asleep, he will recover. We are in good shape (see verse 12). Of course, Jesus had spoken of Lazarus's death, but they understood it as literal sleep (verse 13). Jesus sees the need to explain what He really meant. "So Jesus then said to them plainly, 'Lazarus is dead, and I am glad for your sakes that I was not there, so that you may believe; but let us go to him' " (verses 14, 15). Jesus is glad? So that they may believe? Jesus, how can You say that Lazarus is dead and be glad at the same time? How can we believe when You don't show up on time? Oh, says Jesus, I'm never late; I am always on time. Just believe and you will see My glory! I know the joy I will bring, and you will have the opportunity to believe in Me! Oh, dear Jesus! I believe! Help my unbelief!

Let me make a parenthesis in the narrative. Up to the Christian Era, fear of death was common, paralyzing, and widespread. People were terrified by the very thought of death and the unknown surrounding it. When Jesus lived, died, and conquered death, He radically changed the way His followers spoke about death. It was no longer the horrifying event it previously had been perceived to be, but now it was a sweet sleep instead. The deceased are resting in a sweet sleep, awaiting the resurrection morning when they will hear a loud Voice calling them out of their tombs. Just as Lazarus was. Well, we are jumping ahead in the story. What a difference our faith-in-Jesus glasses make when a loved one dies! We have hope because He conquered death!

The core

When Jesus finally arrives, He finds that Lazarus has been dead for four days (verse 17). This is an important fact because, at that time, some rabbis and their followers believed that the soul of a dead person waited for three days before departing. On the fourth day, they believed, when the body started decomposing, the soul left for good. It is quite interesting to find that the narrative repeatedly stresses the fact that Lazarus had been dead for four days. What it meant to John's audience was that Lazarus was really, really dead.

As previously mentioned, Bethany, the village where Lazarus, Martha, and Mary lived, was less than two miles from Jerusalem (see verse 18), which means that Jesus is coming closer and closer to His own death. "Many of the Jews had come to Mary and Martha, to console them" because of their brother's death (verse 19). The Jewish people believed that consoling the mourning family was a highly regarded duty. They took it very seriously. After allowing the immediate family a time of mourning in solitude, the Jews would come to spend time with them. If you have ever lost a member of your family, you know how important the presence of close friends is, even if the time is spent in silence.

We are focusing on the dialogue between Jesus and Martha. Martha is the active sister (Luke 10:38–42). She is usually the host, the greeter, the server, and seems to be the one in charge. "Martha therefore, when she heard that Jesus was coming, went to meet Him, but Mary stayed at the house" (John 11:20). And this is when the most amazing dialogue about faith takes place. To illustrate the main point of the story, I am going to use an analogy of a layered fruit, such as an orange or a grapefruit. Please imagine a large citrus fruit with three layers: the rind or the outer skin, the white, spongy inner lining, and the juicy pulp, which really is the main part of the fruit that we are after. This fruit represents faith. At least three levels of faith are developed in this narrative. Imagine that you can eat all three layers of our faith fruit. But as you do that, you are getting closer and closer to the juicy and sweet core of the fruit.

First level of belief. When Martha meets Jesus, she becomes very vulnerable; it has been called one of the most vulnerable speeches in the Bible: " 'Lord, if You had been here, my brother would not have died. Even now I know that whatever You ask of God, God will give You' " (verses 21, 22). Martha's statement is more about regret than rebuke, and it reveals a great deal of faith. Martha believes in Jesus' ability to heal, and she still believes that

JOHN

God can hear Jesus even though He apparently missed His healing opportunity. She believes in Jesus' ability to communicate with God. She believes in prayer. There is no indication that Martha foresees a resurrection, only that she believes in Jesus' special connection with God. The word *whatever* in verse 22 is plural, meaning that Martha *knows* that "whatever things" Jesus may ask of God, He would still hear Him. It is interesting to notice that Martha responds with an "I know." I know that prayer works. We will call this first level of faith the *how* of the Christian life: belief in prayer, spiritual disciplines, Bible study, intercessory prayer, and even spiritual gifts. This is important, isn't it? Extremely important. But this is only the beginning, the outer skin of the fruit, the outer layer, very useful, but not what the fruit is all about. Jesus says there is more, much more.

Second level of belief. Jesus answers, " 'Your brother will rise again' " (verse 23). This sentence sounds like a common manner of consolation, something that you and I would say to mourners at a funeral. But Jesus means more than that.

Martha answers Jesus with another "I know" statement: " 'I know that he will rise again in the resurrection on the last day' " (verse 24). The certainty that at the end of the age the dead would rise was a Jewish expectation (see Daniel 12:2). It is exactly what I personally believe; that those who have believed in Christ are now in an unconscious sleep awaiting the Voice that will resurrect them at the end of time. This belief brings me great comfort when someone I love passes away. Martha seems to have her doctrine right; she *knows* that her brother will be resurrected on the last day. We will call this second level of belief the *what* of the Christian faith: doctrinal belief, the white, spongy inner lining of our faith fruit. Is doctrinal belief important? It is super important! This is what the Christian believes. I am a Seventh-day Adventist pastor; our denomination has twenty-eight official doctrines. I believe in these doctrines. But, Jesus says, there is more, much more than doctrines.

Third level of belief. Jesus does not just give life; He is Life. And, therefore, Jesus is trying to help Martha develop an even deeper level of faith—a more profound understanding of who He is, deeper than *how*s and *what*s, as important as they are. Jesus wants Martha to believe in the core: the WHO of the Christian faith. "Jesus said to her, '*I am* the resurrection and the life; he who believes in *Me* will live even if he dies, and everyone who lives and believes in *Me* will never die. Do you *believe* this?' " (John 11:25, 26; emphasis added). Oh, Martha, Martha, you *know* so many things. You know the *how,* you know the *what.* But do you know the *Who*? Do you *believe* in *Me*? "I AM" the very core of the faith fruit, the juice, says Jesus; I am it, I am sweet, I am the Resurrection, I am the Life. And all the *how*s and *what*s are there in order to give you access to the *Who.* They don't stand on their own. And whoever believes in Me will have eternal life. Do you believe this?

And for the first time in the narrative, Martha leaves her "I know" aside, and answers with an "I believe" statement: " 'Yes, Lord; I have *believed* that *You* are the Christ, the Son of God, even He who comes into the world' " (verse 27; emphasis added). Martha responds to Jesus' faith challenge with a threefold answer: (1) She believes that Jesus is the Christ, (2) she believes that Jesus is the Son of God, and (3) she believes that Jesus is One who was to come into the world, the One who fulfills all Jewish Messianic expectations. This belief in Jesus will be greatly tested a few moments later, when Jesus will command that the stone be removed.

I have learned much from this dialogue. I have come to understand that the outer skin and the white inner lining of the fruit are very important—but only as long as they are giving us access to the pulp. I have come to believe that we are not to try to reach people with the *how* and *what* by themselves because they are merely in service of the *Who.* And I do not view doctrines as separate pearls lined up on a string, but rather one great diamond that I can admire from numerous angles. I believe that the *how* and the *what* are a means to an end, which is the *Who.* They *must* be used like straws through which we drink the Living Water, the juice from the core. Taken separately and by themselves, detached from the core, the *how*s and the *what*s will be dry and of no value. The gospel, the good news, is quite simple: whoever believes in Jesus shall be saved. Jesus is the core.

Jesus is the Resurrection

The next dialogue between Jesus and Martha happens at the tomb. After talking with Mary, Jesus asks where they have laid Lazarus (verses 28–33). He is invited to " 'come and see' " (verse 34). The next verse is the shortest verse of the Bible: "Jesus wept." The verb used here is different from the verb for *weep* used elsewhere in this story. The other characters are mourning loudly; Jesus is weeping quietly (this term is used only here in the entire New Testament). He is moved by everyone's sorrow. He knows what He is about to do, but He is touched with the suffering of humanity. I saw a drawing many years ago that is still fresh in my mind—Jesus, reading the newspaper and weeping. God is touched by our suffering even though He knows that He is going to do something about it soon; He is going to exterminate death and evil once and for all.

The Jews interpret Jesus' tears as His expression of love. Others regret the fact that He wasn't there to heal Lazarus the way He healed the blind man of chapter 9 (see John 11:36, 37). Their statement confirms and legitimizes the miracle that had happened, when the Light of the world brought full sight to a man born blind.

As Jesus makes His way to the tomb, the narrator reminds the reader that Lazarus is, in fact, *really* dead. The scene includes a tomb, a stone against it, the sister of the dead man, the fact that four days have gone by, and the warning that the body is decomposing and, therefore, there will be a stench (see verses 38, 39). As if Jesus had not noticed all these signs of death, He gives the most outrageous order: " 'Remove the stone' " (verse 39). Remove the stone?

Martha, the very one who made a confession that Jesus was the Christ, the Son of God (verse 27), objects. She reminds Jesus of a very practical fact; after four days, the body would smell bad. The

King James Version says that Martha reminds Jesus that it "stinketh." What could possibly be a good reason for the removing of the stone? Perhaps Jesus wants to see His friend one last time, but it will do Him no good. He won't be able to recognize him after four days, plus the stench of decay won't be a good memory either.

But this was not the reason why Jesus wanted the stone removed. Didn't I tell you, Martha, that if you believe in Me, " 'you will see the glory of God?' " (verse 40). Believe in Me!

Jesus then prays to His Father. He doesn't ask for power or pray for God to hear His request for a resurrection. He prays for those who are about to witness this climactic miracle, that they might *believe in Him*. Many of those present know their Scriptures, but they do not believe in Him. Jesus prays that they might come to understand that the Father sent Him.

"When He had said these things, He cried out with a loud voice, 'Lazarus, come forth' " (verse 43). Lazarus, come out! Lazarus, Life Himself is calling you!

And the dead man came out.

Many say that Jesus called Lazarus by name because otherwise everyone buried in that cemetery would have come out. Life Himself was calling the dead, and death could not resist Life. Lazarus was bound with wrappings: hands, feet, and face. Jesus then commanded, " 'Unbind him, and let him go' " (verse 44).

Believe

Jesus died to give Lazarus life. Literally. Even though Jesus' prayer was answered and many Jews believed in Him, others went to the Pharisees to tell them what had happened (verses 45, 46). "From that day on they planned together to kill Him" (verse 53). In the Gospel of John, this is the event that triggers Jesus' death. So, in more than one sense, Jesus died so Lazarus could live. The Cross is the glory of the Son of God. This event led to that fateful weekend. Many words in this narrative foreshadow Jesus' death and resurrection: Jerusalem, tomb, stone, wrappings, and so on. Jesus' resurrection would ultimately triumph over death.

This story may also be interpreted on a deeper level as an enacted parable of the coming day of the Lord when all believers will hear a loud Voice ordering them out of the tomb. This narrative highlights the importance of believing in the Person of Jesus as the assurance for eternal life. The worth of the *hows* and the *whats* is measured by their value in the light of the *Who.* Jesus is the Resurrection and the Life. Resurrection and life are not just doctrines: Jesus is Life.

If you are facing the death of a loved one or any other type of tomblike situation, whether emotional, spiritual, or physical, this story brings you hope. The glasses of faith in Jesus allow you to experience "unseen certainties." His love for us guarantees that the end is eternal life for all those who believe in Him because Jesus redeemed us on the cross and conquered death itself.

You have a choice. You can live your life by sight; but let me warn you, it "stinketh." Or you can live your life by faith in the Son of God. If you believe, you will see His glory. These are your two choices. I hope you choose faith over fear. Faith in Jesus is the only way I can live with the assurance of my salvation. When I look at myself, I don't know how I could ever be saved (I stinketh), but when I look at Jesus (putting on my glasses of faith), I don't know how I could ever be lost.

We may be suffering today, and God weeps with us. But the Bible says that He also has a plan: " 'He will dwell among them, and they shall be His people, and God Himself will be among them, and He will wipe away every tear from their eyes; and there will no longer be any death; there will no longer be any mourning, or crying, or pain; the first things have passed away' " (Revelation 21:3, 4).

By the way, when you believe in Jesus, you already know the end of your story. He already wrote it at the cross. This is the unseen certainty you can live with if you have your faith glasses on.

I can't wait for the end of time, when in thunderous voice, Jesus commands the devil, "Unbind them and let them go!"

The Completion

Unfortunately, in a booklet of this size, we must be selective. I wish we had more space to discuss other signs and dialogues such as Jesus and His mother at Cana (John 2:1–11), Jesus and the paralytic at Bethesda (John 5:1–18), Jesus and the crowds (John 6; 7), Jesus and Mary (John 12:1–11), Jesus and His disciples (John 13–17), Jesus with Judas, the priests, and Pilate (John 18), Jesus and Mary Magdalene on Resurrection morning (John 20:1–18), and Jesus and Peter (John 13:1–11; 18:25–27; 21:1–19), to name a few. I hope you take the time to study these dialogues on your own.

This last chapter will be devoted to Jesus' crucifixion and the subsequent dialogue with Thomas after His resurrection. In many ways, all the topics that John has been discussing are summarized in John 19 and 20. The Gospel opens with the beginning before Creation and we end at the completion. Everything Jesus came to do culminates in these two chapters, which end with the author's statement of his purpose in writing this Gospel.

But before we begin this important segment, I must point out a certainty available to you: if you really come to believe in what John presents in this section of the Gospel, you *do have* eternal life. This Gospel has been written so that you may come to believe in the divinity of Jesus and that you may be assured of eternal life that He has secured for you. In times of uncertainty, we all would like to have a road map for our life's journey—a way of knowing that everything is going to be OK. Well, John says to each one of us, If you are a believer in Jesus Christ, then I can tell you the end of your journey. Really, John? Can you give us that much assurance? Absolutely! He says, " 'He who believes in the Son *has* eternal life' " (John 3:36; emphasis added).

The hour has come!

Beginning with the very first miracle of Jesus narrated in this Gospel, the reader has been informed that Jesus knows that His hour will eventually arrive, " 'My hour has not yet come' " (John 2:4). As we move closer to Passover Friday, Jesus becomes aware that His hour has finally arrived; "Now before the Feast of the Passover, Jesus knowing that His hour had come" (John 13:1); " 'Father, the hour has come' " (John 17:1).

Jesus is condemned to die; He will be crucified (John 19:16). The narrator is careful to mention several details. We are told that Jesus carried His own cross (a literal translation of the Greek would read, "carrying the cross for Himself," verse 17). John wants us to understand that Jesus is always in control and submitting Himself to what is going on. Many see in this act of Jesus carrying His own cross the fulfillment of another event, which is recorded in Genesis 22:6, where Isaac, the beloved son of Abraham, carried the firewood of his own sacrifice. I believe that Isaac was indeed a type or symbol of the real Sacrifice, the beloved Son of God.

John 19:17 names the place of the Crucifixion in both Greek ("the Place of a Skull") and Jewish Aramaic ("Golgotha"). The English word *Calvary* comes from the Latin *calvaria,* which also means "skull." Jesus was crucified between two men, one on each side (see verse 18), fulfilling the prophecy given by Isaiah regarding the Suffering Servant:

He poured out Himself to death,
And was numbered with the transgressors;
Yet He Himself bore the sin of many,
And interceded for the transgressors (Isaiah 53:12).

John gives many details not provided by the other Gospels; perhaps because he was a personal eyewitness to the events being narrated here. I can almost hear John singing the line from the spiritual "Were you there when they crucified my Lord?" One of these details is that the sign placed on the cross with the legal charge for Jesus' death was written in three languages: Jewish Aramaic, Latin, and Greek (John 19:20). Everyone who knew how to read could read this sign: "It was written, 'JESUS THE NAZARENE, THE KING OF THE JEWS' " (verse 19). John is also the only Gospel writer to tell us that the Jews objected to the inscription, requesting that it be changed from a fact to a claim. But Pilate would not hear one more word about it (verses 21, 22). It was done. This sign is paradoxical because the Jews had refused to have Jesus as their King (verse 15). It had been the original charge brought against Him (John 18:33), and now it was there for everyone to see. From the Roman perspective, Jesus was dying for sedition or treason. But there is a second reality: through the eyes of faith, the believer knows that the hour had come for Jesus to bear the sins of the world and enter His glory as the King of the universe. He is the King of kings.

In Roman tradition, when a criminal had been condemned, he was placed in the center of a *quaternion,* a company of four soldiers. It was part of their prerogative to divide among themselves the garments of the one crucified. We are told that they made four parts of Jesus' outer garment, one for each. But the tunic, the inner garment, was seamless and would have more value if it remained in one piece. So they cast lots to decide who would get it (verses 23, 24). John even notes that the division of Jesus' clothing fulfilled a prophecy (Psalm 22:18). You might want to take a moment and read all of Psalm 22 and see how many of the words in this psalm foreshadow Jesus' crucifixion as narrated by the four Gospels. Yes, my friend, God was in control. He had even inspired these prophetic words hundreds of years before. Jesus' death was not an accident.

In contrast with the four Roman soldiers who seem unaware of the fact that they are crucifying God, John places these devout women who have followed Jesus to the foot of the cross: Jesus' mother, His aunt, Mary the wife of Clopas, and Mary Magdalene

(John 19:25). Jesus' mother is always unnamed in the Gospel of John. But wait—Jesus is about to speak!

It is finished!

When Jesus sees His mother and the disciple whom He loved (already introduced in John 13:23), He speaks. John records three last sayings of Jesus on the cross that are not recorded by the other Gospel writers. The first one is addressed to His mother and the beloved disciple. It is amazing to me that in the midst of His physical and even greater spiritual distress, Jesus thinks of His mother. His mother was visited by the angel Gabriel, and when she had become pregnant out of wedlock, she endured much ridicule. She had witnessed and personally suffered because of Jesus' rejection by the Jews. She had kept in her heart the prophecies about Him, and now she was standing by the cross of her beloved Son. And Jesus honors His earthly mother by making sure that she is taken care of. Amazing! May we treat our own mothers with such care and tenderness. Jesus' brothers had not yet believed that He was the Savior (John 7:5), so Jesus felt the need to entrust His mother to the beloved disciple: "When Jesus then saw His mother, and the disciple whom He loved standing nearby, He said to His mother, 'Woman, behold, your son!' Then He said to the disciple, 'Behold your mother!' From that hour the disciple took her into his own household" (John 19:26, 27).

Jesus continues to be in control. It was not the nails that kept Jesus on the cross. No! No! It was His love for you and me that kept Him there! He had the power to get down from the cross and avoid additional torture and death. But His love for us was greater than His physical, emotional, and spiritual anguish. John tells us that Jesus knew that at His dying moment all things were accomplished, that His work was finished, and that His mission was consummated. The Greek word expressing completion is *tetelestai* (verse 28). We will encounter this important word again two verses later.

Jesus knows. Yes, Jesus knows that all things are completed and that all Scripture has been fulfilled. He then says, " 'I am thirsty' " (verse 28). He is given vinegar. Even this utterance fulfills a prophecy (Psalm 69:21). This is a different occurrence from the one mentioned in the other Gospels in which He refused the drink because it was mixed with a substance (usually myrrh) designed to numb the pain and offer some relief from His suffering. Jesus wanted to be fully alert for the redemption of the world. For a differentiation between the drinks, the one refused and the one accepted, read about both in Mark 15:23, 36. Jesus is now about to submit His spirit; He is about to die. This drink is not for pain relief but to moisten His throat so that what He is about to say may be heard. This is it. This is the end. Those around Him put the vinegar on a sponge attached to a branch of hyssop. John's inclusion of this detail is significant because at the time of the Exodus, the Israelites dipped twigs of hyssop in the blood of the Passover lamb to mark the lintels and doorposts of the houses of those who were about to be redeemed (see Exodus 12:22). What a fulfillment! Jesus is the Passover Lamb!

After receiving the vinegar (John 19:30), Jesus could now utter the loud cry that would pronounce His mission completed. It was not a victim's agonizing cry of pain; it was a Victor's shout of triumph: " 'It is finished!' " (verse 30). And yes, you guessed it, in Greek the shouted word is *tetelestai*. We had already been told that Jesus knew that everything that He came to do had been accomplished. Now He announces it to the universe: It is done! It is accomplished! It is finished! It is completed!

The salvation of the human race was accomplished and completed two thousand years ago. This is how Christians spell salvation: D-O-N-E.

Jesus then bowed His head and gave up His spirit. He *voluntarily* gave up His spirit. He had designed the plan, and now He had completed it. He consented to His death. And He accomplished redemption for you and me. This was His will and His

Father's will. God chose to rather die than spend eternity without us. Only Christians worship a God who died in their place. Oh, Jesus! How could You love us that much?

To believe or not to believe: That is the question

After Jesus dies, Joseph of Arimathea and Nicodemus take care of His body and place it in an unused tomb. You can read John 19:31–42 for the details. Only in this Gospel are we told that Nicodemus, who had first come to see Jesus at night (chapter 3), is now caring for Jesus' body in broad daylight. Isn't it amazing what happens when we put on our glasses of faith?

On Sunday morning, Mary Magdalene finds that the stone has been removed from Jesus' tomb. She runs and tells Peter and the disciple Jesus loved (John 20:1, 2). Both disciples run to the tomb and find it empty! Jesus had been resurrected from the dead! Jesus had resurrected! Death could not hold Life in its grip. Death was now conquered! Once and for all!

A very interesting detail is found in verse 8; the beloved disciple entered the tomb, "and he saw and believed." The disciples had not yet understood the prophecies concerning Jesus' resurrection. But the beloved disciple "saw and believed." The line from the song is still in my heart: "Were you there when He rose up from the grave?"

The first person to see Jesus is Mary Magdalene. Not only to see Him, but to talk with Him. Can you imagine? Women were not even allowed as witnesses in the courts of law at that time. And the King of the universe chooses Mary Magdalene as His first eyewitness! You can read this gripping story in John 20:1–18. "Mary Magdalene came, announcing to the disciples, 'I have seen the Lord,' and that He had said these things to her" (verse 18). This is a story that the first-century church would never make up because in some ways it would have been embarrassing for them to tell the world that Jesus talked with Mary before He met with His eleven disciples.

But the disciples' turn did come. "So when it was evening on that day, the first day of the week, and when the doors were shut where the disciples were, for fear of the Jews, Jesus came and stood in their midst and said to them, 'Peace be with you' " (verse 19). It is hard to imagine what the disciples felt when they saw Him. All we know is that they rejoiced! (verse 20). Then Jesus commissioned them and gave them the Holy Spirit. What a reunion!

But Thomas wasn't present at that reunion

The other disciples were excited to tell him, " 'We have seen the Lord!' " (verse 25), but they found that Thomas was skeptical. He wanted to see for himself: "he said to them, 'Unless I see in His hands the imprint of the nails, and put my finger into the place of the nails, and put my hand into His side, I will not believe' " (verse 25). This is the only place in all four Gospels that informs us that nails were used in Jesus' crucifixion. There was more than one method to hang a body on the cross. John records that Thomas demanded to see the imprint of the nails.

Thomas, the twin, is an interesting character (his Aramaic and Greek names are given here). He is a loyal but pessimistic disciple (see 11:16; 14:5). To him, the Cross was only what he had expected; he even suggested that the disciples go with Jesus to Jerusalem in order to die with Him (John 11:16). Perhaps now he is mourning alone, repeating to himself, *I knew it! I knew it!* Now he is demanding a visual and kinesthetic proof; he will believe only when he can see and touch. No one mentioned in the entire New Testament makes greater demands in order to believe. This is why Thomas became the epitome of unbelief. Sight not faith!

In all fairness, before we judge Thomas too harshly, we have to realize that he is only asking for the same evidence that everyone else already had. After all, the ten also believed because they saw. We are even told of the beloved disciple that "he saw and believed" (John 20:8). One of the great drawbacks of unbelief is that your joy is delayed! Thomas could have been rejoicing with the rest; but, because he refused to believe, he had to wait for another week. His unbelief delayed his joy. What about us? Would you believe even if you didn't see? Would faith have prevailed in me?

Eight days later, the disciples were together again. This time Thomas was with them. The episode is narrated in the same way as in Jesus' first appearance to His disciples. The doors are shut, and all of a sudden Jesus appears in their midst and says, " 'Peace be with you' " (verse 26). By the way, I find it so comforting that Jesus always speaks of peace when He shows up. I have come to believe that peace is the presence of Christ—even in the midst of trouble.

Jesus immediately addresses Thomas: " 'Reach here with your finger, and see My hands; and reach here your hand and put it into My side; and do not be unbelieving, but believing' " (verse 27). Wow! This is what you requested, Thomas! Come! Wouldn't you like to have God show up with the proof you requested? Jesus' words show that He is completely aware of Thomas's demands even though He had not been present when Thomas made them. But at the sight of Jesus, Thomas forgets all about his required proof and immediately puts on the glasses of faith and expresses the most profound confession that we find in all four Gospels: "Thomas answered and said to Him, 'My Lord and my God!' " (verse 28). Nobody has ever addressed Jesus like this. Thomas has made a leap of faith and has come to believe that Jesus is God, thereby, confirming John's assertion at the very beginning of the Gospel: "In the beginning was the Word, and the Word was with God, and the Word was God. . . . The Word became flesh" (John 1:1, 14). The Gospel has become a full circle. God became flesh, died to accomplish our salvation, and rose from the dead. Do you believe that?

Jesus then gives His last beatitude: "Jesus said to him, 'Because you have seen Me, have you believed? Blessed are they who did not see, and yet believed' " (John 20:29). From then on, belief on the basis of sight would no longer be available. Living on the basis of faith would be the only way. And blessed are those who, since then, have come to believe without seeing. This is the reason why the Gospel of John was written—that we may believe.

Conclusion

"Therefore many other signs Jesus also performed in the presence of the disciples, which are not written in this book; but these have been written so that you may believe that Jesus is the Christ, the Son of God; and that believing you may have life in His name" (verses 30, 31). There we have it! John's statement of purpose.

This Gospel was not written so that we may have an exhaustive biography of Jesus. It was not written so that we may have every detail of His life and every sign that He performed. It was written so that we may believe!

The truth we need to believe is twofold: (1) Jesus is who He says He is, and (2) He has done what He says He has done. John wrote so that we may believe in Jesus' identity and what He has accomplished on our behalf: Jesus is God and He has purchased eternal life for us. This is His glory: *tetelestai*! It is completed! It is finished!

So, let's put on our glasses of faith in Jesus and live our lives with the assurance of salvation. Even when we have to go through things in life that "stinketh," our faith in Jesus will allow us to behold His glory, to be certain of realities not seen, the most important one being our own salvation. Believe! " 'He who believes in the Son has eternal life' " (John 3:36).

God became flesh that we may have abundant life. Jesus says, " 'I came that they may have life, and have it abundantly' " (John 10:10). Believe it! It's true!

After all, since *The Beginning* He has been *The Antidote* offered to us in *The Exchange* in which He took upon Himself *The Verdict* becoming *The Light* that illuminated our darkness, and gave us *The Life* that He purchased at the cross through His blood in *The Completion* of His mission! And here you have it, all the titles of the chapters of this booklet—we have completed our journey too.

Believe in the Son and live! This is the purpose of the Gospel of John, and it is the purpose of my writing as well.

So, how do you like the 3-D picture?

Faith glasses, anyone?

If you have been blessed by this booklet and would like to help us keep spreading the good news of Jesus Christ through preaching, teaching, and writing, please send your donations to

Voice of Prophecy
Attn: Jesus101 Biblical Institute
P. O. Box 941659
Simi Valley, CA 93094

www.vop.com